Dorothy Stanley

London Street Arabs

Dorothy Stanley

London Street Arabs

ISBN/EAN: 9783744752473

Printed in Europe, USA, Canada, Australia, Japan

Cover: Foto ©ninafisch / pixelio.de

More available books at **www.hansebooks.com**

Yours sincerely
Dorothy Stanley

BY

Mrs. H. M. STANLEY

(DOROTHY TENNANT.

CASSELL & COMPANY, LIMITED:

LONDON, PARIS & MELBOURNE.

1890.

BY WAY OF INTRODUCTION.

..

I CANNOT remember my first ragamuffin drawing. There has always been a strange affinity between me and the London "gamin." Born in London, fond of walking through its streets, parks, and squares, the first interesting object I must have seen was doubtless some dear little child in tatters; and as I loved drawing even more than I loved the ragamuffin, it was quite natural for me to try and "make a picture of him."

My first serious essay was a set of "Scenes in Seven Dials." In my childish imagination Seven Dials meant the home of the ragamuffin, and I entreated in vain to be taken there for my morning walk. I next remember illustrating "Passages from the Life of Jack Sheppard," and resolving in my own mind that when I grew up I should be the champion painter of the poor, and, of course, a very great artist indeed.

Most of the pictures I had seen of ragged life appeared to me false and made up. They were all so deplorably piteous—pale, whining children with sunken eyes, holding up bunches of violets to heedless passers-by; dying match-girls, sorrowful water-cress girls, emaciated mothers clasping weeping babes. How was it, I asked myself, that the other side is so seldom represented? The merry, reckless, happy-go-lucky urchin; the tom-boy girl; the plump, untidy mother dancing and tossing her ragged baby;

who had given this side of London life? Murillo's "Beggar Boys" most nearly approached my ideal—but *where* was the modern Murillo? Surely there is material for the painter in our parks, our streets, our Embankment by the banks of the Thames. Oh! the pictures on Bank Holiday in Battersea Park, or in St. James's Park! The pretty scenes of courting and playing, the girls lying on the grass, the babies tumbling over them, mopheaded boys playing at cricket, the groups at the fountains—every day, every hour, there are pictures worth painting to be seen in or about London. Why go to Venice when we have such pictures at home? Stand in Endell Street and watch the little fountain not far from the Baths and Workhouse—just too high for the baby, who is just too heavy for the little brother or sister to lift. What an upheaving and struggling before the water trickles over the lips and down the neck—down, over the ragged frock, into the very boots which gape so wide at the ankle! How I wish I could draw them as I see them, as I feel them—but there is such a wide chasm between conceiving and carrying out. No ragamuffin is ever vulgar or common. If the pictures render him so, it is the artist's fault, since he always puts himself into his work. All his vulgarity and affectations go into the drawing, just as simplicity, dignity, and love of truth are to be found in the work if found in the artist.

What everlasting laurels a really great artist might win for himself, merely by painting London! Hogarth loved the ragamuffin and the Londoner, and has told us the story of his day better than any book can tell it. It is not so very difficult, if you are gifted to start with, and are *meant* to be a painter. You must first walk about little back streets and alleys towards sunset; stroll round the lake in St. James's Park, or along the Embankment by the steps leading down to the water. Saturday is the best day, of course. Then look, and look without worrying your mind to remember; take it all in—the movements, the groups, the attitudes—without troubling yourself much as to detail.

Of an evening, sit at a table with a good lamp, pencil and paper, and let your pencil do what it likes. After a while something will take shape, probably a vague recollection of your walks — just like the incoherent jumble of a dream. Then you wake up and begin to compose with a little more method. The boy carries a baby on his back, and stops to talk with a girl driving a heavily-laden old perambulator. A row of urchins sit along the kerb, their feet in the gutter, enjoying the cool mud, so soft and grateful after the hot asphalte pavements.

Picture after picture comes of itself, and if one of the sketches particularly takes your fancy, you rise the next morning with a glowing determination to " set to work " without loss of time. Perhaps the necessary ingredients of your picture are a red-headed boy, and a fair curly-headed boy, a small girl and a big baby, and an old hamper. All these have to be found and brought home. One must not be too exacting about the colour and style of hair and dress, etc. The best thing is to keep your properties in the studio. A good supply of rags is essential (carefully fumigated, camphored, and peppered), and you can then dress up your too respectable ragamuffin till he looks as disreputable as you can wish.

If you have no rags to start with, and shrink from keeping them *by* you, the best way is to find an average boy, win his confidence, give him sixpence, and promise him another sixpence if he will bring you a boy more ragged than himself. This second boy must be invited to do the same, and urged to bring one yet more "raggety." You can in this way get down to a very fine specimen, but the drawback is the loss of time caused by the cajoling, the difficulty of explaining what you want and why you want it, and the great probability of failure after all your expenditure of time, eloquence, and sixpences. It *is* disheartening to find Joey Brown who promises to bring Tommy Gedge—describing him as " raggety all over:" a boy " wot never washes hisself,"—after two hours' waiting, arrive triumphant, dragging reluctant Tommy, shy and overcome by his own magnificence and cleanliness, in a 3s. 6d. suit, stiff sailor hat, face shining with soap and cocoanut oil which drips from his smoothed hair. Joey walks round his friend in the deepest admiration, trying to soothe his envy by remarking that " them sort of boots don't wear," and that " the buttons look well enough at first, but the tops drop off that there kind, only leaving the shanks." Here, if you have by you a good supply of old "cords" (corduroy trousers) and a very ragged shirt, a length of worn or "chewed" string for braces, and an old boot, Tommy can be made to look himself again; he will probably weep, but that helps to make his face dirty, and is therefore to be slightly encouraged. The hair is the chief drawback, but it *can* be worried up into a mop again if vigorously shampooed by his friend. And *there* you have your model quite ready!

But you must remember that Tommy will never reappear after that first sitting unless you can manage not only to soothe his wounded vanity, but also to keep him well amused and to excite pleasurable expectation for the next sitting. On the first day, therefore, very little work is done. You must make Tommy's acquaintance, study "his lines," and "take him in" as well as you can. He will probably fall into attitudes which will serve for future sketches, and which probably will come out in the evening scribbles. The time therefore is not altogether lost, though very little actual work is done.

An old piano is very attractive to ragamuffins. Mine was rendered prematurely old by the children. Not so very long ago it was quite a smart well-toned piano, now its pedals are irresponsive. The ivory has dropped or been picked off the notes, and the white keys are smudged over by small black finger marks. Ragamuffins are almost always loyal; they invariably ask to play "God save our gracious Queen." Tommy or Jimmy, Hetty or Betsy, they all must play that tune. "Please Miss, may I be learned 'God save our gracious Queen'?" The process of teaching is simple though monotonous. You take the ragamuffin's fore-finger, which is unduly stiffened, and direct it to each note with a thump. (The wrist and arm of the ragamuffin invariably appear to be paralysed.) You repeat this at every rest, perhaps for a week, and then he can remember it for himself. I do not know which is worse—to teach him or to hear him hammer it out for himself.

The last boy I taught asked me whether the "pianner would play any other tune." "No," I replied, with much decision, fearing I might be called upon to teach him "God bless the Prince of Wales," or "Rule Britannia." One small boy—Jimmie Moore—was most anxious to learn

"Rule Britannia," because he "knowed the words;" and this was his rendering, faithfully recorded at the time :—

> "Rule Britallion,
> Britallion ruins the whales;
> True 'earted Brittuns
> Never—never shall be slain."

Of all my models, babies of course are the most trying. The young mother generally insists on bringing the infant, and I have to soothe it and endure the mother, who makes the most of her time by telling pitiful stories of conjugal troubles, maternal anxieties, and the cruelty of land-lords. As for the baby, after wriggling about convulsively in a paroxysm of rage, it settles down to sleep in an arm-chair, insisting on being completely shrouded in its mother's shawl, and refusing to allow so much as its toe to appear. I really think the best way to draw babies is to go out for a walk, determined to shut your eyes to everything but babies. For half-an-hour, study the average of babies' arms; then take the average of mouths and noses—the way their pinafores get huddled up— the way their socks run down into their heavy little laced boots, etc. etc. After two hours' walk on the Surrey side of London, one ought to come back learned in babies. It is quite a beautiful study the back of babies' heads— the nape of the neck where the curls lie like gold tendrils, or where the down of early babyhood softly follows the outline of the head.

After all, walking along the streets you can learn far more than in your studio. Which of us could draw a hansom cab from recollection, or an omnibus? You would find it necessitated many a walk along the Strand, Oxford Street, Holborn, or any great thoroughfare. You would have to stare at the lamps, the shafts, the curve of the top, the seat of the driver many a time before you could draw them.

It would puzzle you to draw a policeman's helmet, and you would probably make his summer coat too long or his winter coat too short. It would take you some time to master the fact that the policeman has seven plated buttons, that his belt has a snake-like clasp, that his helmet has a particular curve at the back. You must examine him very closely —so closely, indeed, that he will examine *you* suspiciously.

But one is rewarded for all the trouble. The more you look the better you draw, and when you have done your work, the little model always interests or amuses you. He tells you true stories, and makes deep observations ; he confides in you, and wishes to please you ; so that after a while you find yourself attached to Tommy Jones, or Freddy Scott, and you confide *in him*, and even consult him, his opinion of your work being by no means to be despised, since he frequently improves the picture by suggesting modifications in the attitudes.

One boy, Tommy Raper, once helped me out of a difficulty. I wanted a small sweep ; he must be covered with soot, only his eyes and teeth glittering : but where to find him ? I sighed as I thought of the difficulty—the many walks I must take and the many inquiries I must make before I should find my sweep ! Tommy came to the rescue ; if I would give him "a rest" so that he might consider !—and forthwith he retired to my little sitting-room, which opens into the studio. Some time having elapsed, and Tommy's ominous silence making me fear he was up to some mischief, I hastily went in search of him and found his feet in the grate and his body up the chimney !

My Persian rug was thickly covered with soot when Tommy emerged from the chimney, as black and sweeplike as I could desire. Such devotion to art (or to me) could not be greeted by a scolding, though the Persian rug *was* spoilt ; so I painted my sweep, and thanked him for putting himself to so much discomfort on my account.

I could quote many instances of ragamuffin goodwill and ingenuity, but this is not an article or essay I am writing, it is merely an introduction—a "few words"—to accompany these little ragamuffin drawings, so that long anecdotes would be quite out of place. I will say good-bye to the ragamuffin by quoting a few of his definitions, as they give some insight into the mind of the little animal, and show how difficult it is for us to understand them or be understood by them.

I asked a little girl how she would define *love*. Unhesitatingly she replied, "It's going errands."

I asked a boy the meaning of the word *guilt*. "It means telling on another boy."

I asked Harry Sullivan to define a *gentleman.* He replied, not without some fervour, "Oh! a fellow who has a watch and chain."

I suppose he read disapprobation in my face, for he hastily added, "And loves Jesus."

This same boy had a very hazy idea of Old Testament history. He had heard of Adam and Eve—"They stole apples and were turned out of the *gardin,* and then they had to work for their living till the sweat poured down."

A girl of eleven told me how she wished to live in the country, "because then I shouldn't see a lot of people having a lot of things I can't have."*

A dear little boy of six told me he loved Christmas Day because on Christmas Eve he hung up his stocking, and the next morning he found a present inside. "What did you find last Christmas?" I inquired. "A halfpenny," he said, smiling with pleasure at the recollection, "but," he added truthfully, "I put it in myself over-night."

"Boy Taylor," as they call him, has most agreeable stories of his *monster experiences* when he appeared as a Green Demon or Dragon last Christmas at Sanger's Circus. The boys got inside the dragons with some squeezing, and once there they had to pull various strings which made the wings flap and the jaws open. The dragons were then turned into the arena. "I could jist see the elefint's legs by looking through the dragon's mouth, but we couldn't see much, and they didn't let us come afterwards to look at the show." Taylor's dragon career was cut short by too much exuberance of spirits in the green-room. So he "got the sack," and lost four shillings a week; but he was a philosophical youth of nine. "You see I can allus *say* I was a dragon once, and I *did* see the elefint's legs and heard the clown without paying nuffin." And he probably consoled himself by reflecting that looking at elephants' legs every night became monotonous, and that even the clown's jokes grew stale. I found Taylor's dragon experience made him very quick at catching an attitude; indeed he was so fond of his power of endurance that he

* This is rather different from the boy who told me that the advantage of possessing nothing was that "you hadn't anything on your mind."

begged me to paint a boy standing on his head, assuring me that he preferred that attitude to any other.

And now I *will* end, because there seems no reason why I *should* end. The little ragamuffins of my acquaintance have told me many and many a quaint or droll story, but they somehow lose their fun when they are put down in print, just as the grace and charm of the children's attitude are partly lost in the drawings. The pictures that have been gathered together in this volume are illustrations done at different times for different stories which have appeared in *Little Folks*, *The Quiver*, etc. I will just add that the picture of the "Mer-baby" has been included at the request of many friends who are so kind as to express a certain liking for it.* The bairns in this drawing have, obviously, nothing to do with London or streets; but, after all, they *are* ragamuffin though unclothed.

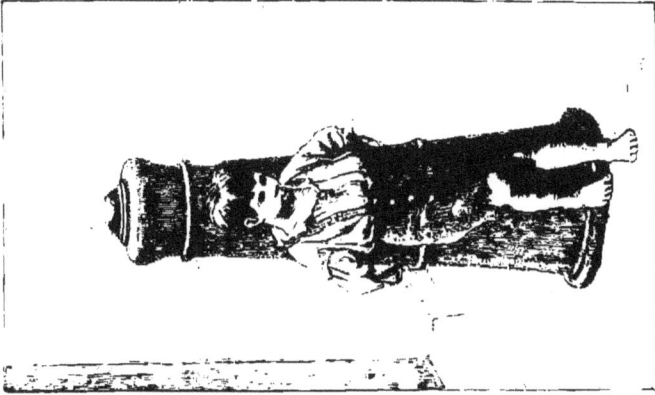

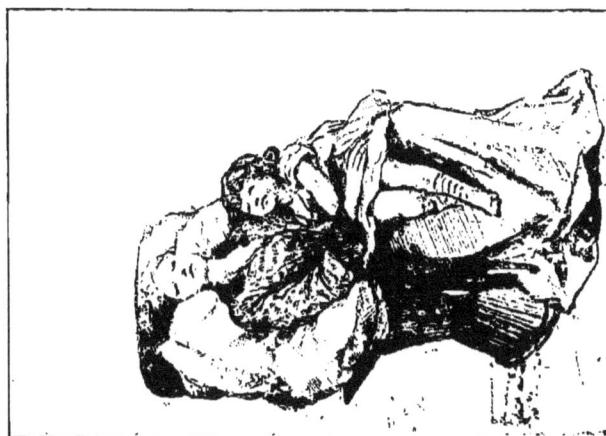

Dorothy Tennant. 88

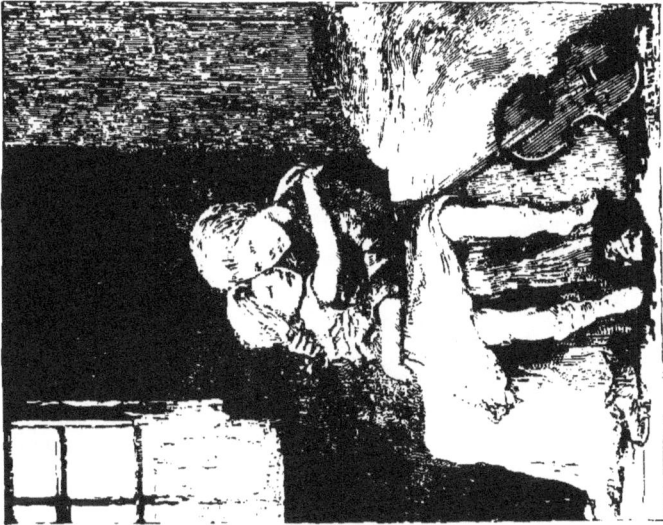

Dorothy Tennant. 96

OUT OF WORK